Y0-CCN-061

50 Ways to a Better You

FOR

DUMMIES®

MINI EDITION

by W. Doyle Gentry, PhD

WILEY

John Wiley & Sons, Inc.

50 Ways to a Better You For Dummies®, Mini Edition

Published by
John Wiley & Sons, Inc.
111 River St.
Hoboken, NJ 07030-5774
www.wiley.com

WILEY

Introduction

*H*appiness is an important part of life — no less than anger, sadness, and fear. It begins with life itself: What mother doesn't recognize the look of happiness on the face of her newborn? Human beings are wired with an innate, neurological potential for happiness, but whether this potential eventually becomes a reality depends on how we choose to live our lives. In other words, happiness isn't an accident, and it isn't a gift from the gods — it's the gift you give yourself!

If you're like me, you're far too passive when it comes to experiencing happiness. You wait for it to find you instead of exercising your right to pursue it. It's *because* most people are passive when it comes to happiness that happiness seems so elusive! Face it: We live in proactive times. People around the world don't *wait* for freedom — they fight for it. Wealth is no longer something you have to inherit — you can *create* it. People are living longer these days. Why? Because we're learning that we can improve quality of life through the everyday choices we make. This little book tells you how to fight for, create, and live a long and happy life. It makes you the master of your own happy destiny!

Icons Used in This Book

Icons are those little pictures in the margins throughout this book that are there to draw your attention to certain types of information.

This icon suggests practical how-to strategies for achieving happiness.

This icon alerts you to important ideas and concepts that you'll want to remember and that you can use when you don't have this book in hand.

This icon appears when I think a cautionary note is in order or when you need to seek professional help.

Where to Go from Here

The first chapter gives you an overview of what it means to be happy. You want to be a better you in order to be happy, no? The next chapter offers 50 tips that you can use to improve yourself. Feel free to skim that chapter or read it from front to back.

Chapter 1

The Search for Happiness

. . . .

In This Chapter

▶ Understanding individual happiness

▶ Discovering common elements in happy people

. . . .

*H*appiness is everywhere — in every country, culture, big city, jungle, canyon, and apartment building in the world, anywhere that human beings reside. Thus, happiness — along with anger, curiosity, fear, disgust, and sadness — is considered a universal emotion.

But some people have a hard time defining happiness in thier lives. This chapter can help.

Happiness from the Individual Perspective

Other people are the best teachers, no matter what you're trying to learn. So, if you want to know how to be happy, what better way to start than by asking people who show happiness more than most people?

Happy people tend to share these common elements:

- ✔ They all attribute much of their happiness to the influences of significant others in their lives (parents, life partners).

- ✔ They all profess a belief that happiness is something you have to work for — you have to find it, it doesn't come looking for you.

- ✔ They all believe it's possible to be happy even when life doesn't always go the way you want it to (for example, when dealing with aging parents, coping with depression, or grieving the loss of loved ones to debilitating illnesses).

- ✔ They all believe in a higher power and practice their religion, and they think that helps them have a positive outlook on life.

- ✔ They all believe in beginning and ending the day with positive thoughts that lend themselves to happiness.

- ✔ They all believe that happiness insures good health and keeps you looking young.

- ✔ They all believe that happiness is something that increases with age (see the following section).

The Demographics of Happiness

Happiness is a very democratic emotion — it isn't an emotion that's available to only a certain group of individuals and not others. But there *are* some demographic characteristics that increase your chances of being happy. I cover these in the following sections.

Age

Age seems to increase a person's overall likelihood of being happy. If you think that young people have the advantage here, you're wrong. Most young people are happy to be sure, but research shows that you're much *more* likely to experience happiness the older you get. In one survey, 38 percent of respondents aged 68 to 77 reported feeling "very happy" as compared to only 28 percent of respondents between the ages of 18 and 27. This same survey showed a sharp increase in happiness scores beginning at age 45 and continuing into the mid-70s. (There was a similar decline in negative emotions with age.)

So, why do people tend to get happier as they get older?

✔ **Older people have reached a point of *satiation* in life.** They've had a sufficient amount of success and positive experiences to feel both grateful and content. Younger people are on the way, but they're not there yet.

✔ **Age alters a person's expectations.** Somewhere along the way, you realize that you don't get everything you want out of life and that life never was meant to be perfect. I tell people all the time, "If you want to be happy, you don't have to like the way life is — you just have to accept that it is that way."

✔ **With age comes *wisdom* — a perspective that results from a combination of accumulated worldly experience and knowledge — not often seen as people muddle through the first half of life.**

It's no coincidence that the people I interviewed (see the preceding section) were all between the ages of 56 and 74.

Marital status

Marriage also seems to make a difference in people's happiness. Married people, generally speaking, are happier than those who are unmarried. This is true for both men and women. Marriage is one of the meaningful social ties. It brings coherence to people's lives, gives them an opportunity to be less selfish, and allows them to tend and befriend those they love.

 Although most of the research looks at happiness in married people, I think it's fair to say that these same benefits would accrue from other types of committed, long-term relationships as well.

Doing the following leads to a successful marriage:

- ✔ Understanding that being in an intimate relationship means being your partner's companion

- ✔ Creating a sense of equity and parity in the relationship

- ✔ Sharing interests, passion, and intimacy

- ✔ Avoiding contempt even when angry

- ✔ Practicing empathy

- ✔ Saying the magic words: "I am sorry."

Education level

The more education you have, the happier you're likely to be. This may be an indirect effect of the positive relationship that education has on a person's earning power, health, ability to cope with the stresses and strains of everyday life, and longevity. In short, education doesn't guarantee that you'll be happy, but it sure does increase your odds.

 Sign up for a class or two at your local community college. Trust me, you'll be happy you did.

Chapter 2

50 Tips for Self Improvement

* *

In This Chapter

▶ Working toward finding happiness in your life

▶ Discovering common elements in happy people

* *

Stuck in a rut? Not sure where to turn? Looking to make your life better? The following 50 tips can help.

1. Talk to Someone

Talk to a happy person you know and see if you can find out what his secret to happiness is. If you're like me, you'll be surprised at how willing he is to talk about why he's happy, who in his life enabled him to feel this way, and what he sees as the benefits that come from always being positive.

2. Broaden Your Focus and Expand Your Thinking

Positive emotions — curiosity, love, joy, contentment, wonder, excitement — expand your focus of attention. When you're angry, your focus narrows to the source of your frustration and the object of your wrath. Your mind is like a heat-seeking missile, bent on destruction.

3. Linger in the Moment

Bottom line: Some people allow time in their busy day for a few moments of happiness, and others don't. Which kind of person are you?

4. Remember That Timing Is Everything

Maybe happiness is meant to be the *exception* rather than the *rule*. If you're happy too much of the time, you might get too comfortable — too complacent — with the way things are and not want to change anything. For example, if people had been happy having to light their homes with candles, we wouldn't have needed Thomas Edison to come along and invent the electric light bulb. If in the Old West, people had been happy with the Pony Express as the major communication link between east and west, we wouldn't have needed the telegraph, telephone, and eventual global telecommunication networks. If Americans had been happy using horses to plow their fields and take them into town, Henry Ford would never have brought us tractors and automobiles.

This could also explain why people tend to be happier as they grow older. Maybe it makes sense that young people are more frustrated, angrier, and more restless about life — these feelings provide the energy necessary to make things happen in terms of productivity, entrepreneurship, creativity, and invention.

What I'm suggesting is that perhaps happiness is wasted on the young and is an emotion better suited to people in the second half of life. Why else would 38 percent of people between the ages of 68 and 77 report being "very happy" as compared to only 28 percent of those between 18 and 27?

Look on the bright side: If you're under age 40, you have something to look forward to — a happier time of life. If you're over 40, good news: You're already well on your way to compounding a life of happiness.

5. Gather Four Basic Ingredients

The foundation for true happiness consists of four basic ingredients: a feeling of safety, a sense of satiation, a sense of perspective, and quietude.

These four ingredients are essential if your goal is happiness. You can't make chicken soup or chicken salad without chicken to start with. But your neighbor may put things in his chicken salad that you can't imagine putting in yours.

6. Don't Overlook Pleasure in Your Life

Make a list of as many things as you can think of that please you. Now ask yourself this crucial question: When was the last time I was *being* that person or *doing* those things?

7. Be Grateful

Begin each new day of your life with a few minutes of quiet reflection about all the things you have to be grateful for, and then, either silently to yourself or out loud, say thank-you for each item on the list. Trust me, there's no better way to start your day and open yourself up to the possibility of happiness.

8. Strive for Serenity

Serenity has to do with peace of mind. Happiness can't find its way into a mind cluttered by worry, anxieties, anger, stress, and who knows what else. Quietude is about finding a quiet *place;* serenity is about having a quiet *mind.* Of course, you'll have an easier time finding serenity in a place of quietude.

Meditation is an excellent way to find serenity. Pick up a copy of *Meditation For Dummies,* 2nd Edition, by Stephan Bodian (Wiley), to get started.

9. Be Well by Looking After Your Well-Being

Common sense will tell you that it's easier to be happy when you're feeling healthy or well than it is to feel happy when you're sick. (Of course, it isn't impossible for human beings to experience happiness when they're not well — it's just more difficult.)

10. Don't Expect Money to Buy Happiness

I'm not here to tell you that money doesn't matter. It does. But it doesn't buy happiness. Money *does* buy physical comfort; emotional and informational support;

and all kinds freedom. Sure, those things are great, but they aren't everything. And plenty of people have those things and aren't the least bit happy.

11. Don't Look for Transforming Experiences

I wish I could tell you that one moment of happiness can transform your life from what it is now to something much better, but I can't. Happiness is an emotion, and emotions are, by definition, short-lived — they come and go like waves on a beach. You're happy, excited, joyful one minute — and the next minute, you're not.

 Happiness occurs in moments, not hours, days, weeks, months, or years. Sometimes the experience lasts just a few seconds; other times it lasts as long as a few minutes. But inevitably it disappears. The trick is to enjoy the moment, to relish the experience, and to be mindful that it'll be gone before you know it. What I do in this book is show you how to create and have more of these moments than you ever have before.

12. Don't Be Afraid to Be Happy

Negative emotions can be toxic. Prolonged sadness — for example, over the death of a loved one — can lead to a state of depression, which can itself be life-threatening. (Depression is linked to the development of heart disease and is a risk factor for heart attacks.)

Too much fear can cause people to become house-bound (a condition known as *agoraphobia,* which means "fear of public places"), have unrelenting headaches, and develop ulcers and high blood pressure.

The good news is that positive emotions, including happiness, aren't toxic. You can't be too happy. So if you find yourself in a happy moment, be thankful for it, and hope it continues beyond 25 minutes!

The next time you find yourself having a happy moment, rate how intense that feeling is on a 10-point scale (where 1 is barely happy and 10 is ecstatic) and time yourself to see how long that feeling lasts. The happier you are, the longer it should last.

13. Be in Sync with Your Surroundings

Your emotions are affected by the world you live in — your physical and social surroundings. If you're in sync with that world, you have a much better chance of achieving happiness.

Think about where you currently live. Now, ask yourself whether you're living in a place where you can be happy. If the answer is yes, then you know that your environment is not the root of your unhappiness. If the answer is no, it might be. If that's the case, you may consider a "geographic cure" — move to that sunny climate you long for during the winter or a city in which you'd be hard pressed to feel bored.

14. Stick with the Right People

Think about the people who are around you — your neighbors, co-workers, family, and friends. Are you living around people who make you happy? If so, then you know for sure that people aren't the reason you're unhappy. If not, try making some new friends or looking for happiness outside of work or your neighborhood. There's no law that says you can't move back closer to your family if that'll make you happy.

15. Do the Right Things

Ask yourself whether you're doing things that make you happy. If you answered yes, then it's a no-brainer: Keep doing those things. If you answered no, try out some new activities — including some of those that I mention in the preceding paragraph.

Look at what you're doing — all the activities of your life (from work to fun and everything in between) — and ask yourself, "Why?" Are you doing things with and for other people for the right reasons? If you answered yes, there's nothing to change. And if you answered no, you need to come up with another reason for doing the same thing — for example, "I want to go to my kid's ball games so he'll have some positive memories of me when I'm no longer around" or "Golf is a great form of exercise — a lot easier than going to a gym and killing myself on the treadmill."

16. Never Pass Up an Opportunity

You may not realize it, but life provides you with lots of opportunities for constructive change — the chance to correct things and get it right.

What determines whether change represents an opportunity or a curse is not the change itself, but rather what you do as a result of the change. If you get fired from a job you hate, and you decide to find another job that's more to your liking, your life will be a lot happier. If you choose, instead, to find another job just like the one you lost, you won't be happier. It's really up to you.

 Take a few minutes to think about your life and ask yourself, "How many opportunities have I had to change my life for the better?" Try to picture each of these times in your mind and remember exactly how you responded to those opportunities. Were they missed opportunities or did you turn your life in a new direction? Maybe you missed these opportunities because you were too pessimistic about the future or you were thinking of these situations as catastrophes rather than opportunities. If you're the type of person who has, in the past, made good use of forced opportunities (ones that you wouldn't have chosen for yourself), then you're in good shape for dealing with whatever comes your way next.

17. Embrace Optimism

Why does optimism matter? Because if your *future* looks rosy, being happy in the *present* is easier.

Beyond the simple reality that optimists are happier people (and happiness is what you're striving for), optimism has other benefits as well:

✔ **Optimists enjoy a greater degree of academic success than pessimists do.** Because optimistic students think it's possible for them to make a good grade, they study hardier and they study smarter. They manage the setting in which they study (choosing the library over the dorm room) and they seek help from others (fellow students, teachers) when they need it. (Optimism, it turns out, is almost as predictive of how well students do in college as the SAT — another reason not to be discouraged if you didn't knock the socks off the SAT.)

✔ **Optimists tend to set more specific goals than pessimists do (for example, "I want to increase my sales by 20 percent this year").** The more specific and concrete your goals are, the more likely you'll be to achieve success. The optimistic student has a goal of making a B+ average this semester; the pessimistic student simply wants to "do well" in school. Similarly, when it comes to achieving happiness, you're better off having goals such as "I want to engineer a better balance between work and play" or "I want to double the number of uplifting experiences I have week in and week out" than something as non-specific as "I want to be happy."

- ✔ **Optimists are more self-confident than pessimists are.** They believe in *themselves* more than fate. (They also bet on themselves more than they bet on the horses!)

- ✔ **Optimists persist and persevere.** They're not quitters!

- ✔ **Optimists welcome second chances after they fail more than pessimists do.** Optimistic golfers always take a *mulligan* (a redo swing without penalty). Why? Because they expect to achieve a better result the second time around.

- ✔ **Optimists are less likely to blame others for their misfortune than pessimists are.** When you blame someone else for your troubles, what you're really saying is, "You're the *cause* of my problem and, therefore, you have to be the *solution* as well." Optimists have just as many troubles as pessimists throughout life — they just accept more responsibility for dealing with their misfortune.

- ✔ **Optimists cope with stress better than pessimists do.** Pessimists worry, optimists act. A patient with coronary heart disease who is pessimistic "hopes and prays" that he doesn't have another heart attack anytime soon. The optimistic heart patient leaves little to chance — instead, he exercises regularly, practices his meditation exercises, adheres to a low-cholesterol diet, and makes sure he always gets a good night's sleep. (Cardiologists love optimistic patients!)

Optimism *rocks* when it comes to . . . well, when it comes to *everything* in life, from your health to your social relationships. Its benefits truly can't be exaggerated or overestimated!

18. Fight Negative Expectations

Pessimism is a learned response, and you don't have to think that way. You learned to expect the worst, and you can unlearn it too. Here are five simple rules to help you do just that:

- **Accept the fact that you're a pessimist at heart.** You don't have to go around sharing that information with just anyone, but you should be honest with yourself about the challenge you face in becoming a more positive-thinking person.

- **Accept the fact that your first thought is always a negative one — that's just a given.** But don't go with this thought, don't dwell on it, and certainly don't let it guide your behavior at that moment.

- **Remember that it's the second thought that counts.** Learn to counteract your initial pessimism by substituting an optimistic thought. So, for example, "I'm not sure I can do this" becomes "Wow, what a great opportunity!"

- **Separate the past from the present (and the future).** Start saying, "That was then; this is now." No longer link the chaos of your early years (or whatever negative experiences you had in the past) with the expectations you have for things that come up in today's world.

- **Reward yourself for this self-initiated change in thinking.** Give yourself a pat on the back, or head to your local coffee shop for your favorite drink.

19. Move Beyond Pessimism

If you've figured out that you're a pessimist, what can you do to change that? Lots! Here are my recommendations:

✔ **Don't fight it — *change* it.** You have to begin by accepting, not resisting, the reality that you always start out with negative thoughts. Resistance is a waste of energy. The more you resist something, the more it persists — try not thinking about the word *elephant* and see what happens. All you can think about now are elephants! The key here is to change the way you think.

✔ **Turn your thoughts around so that you never end with a negative.** For example, instead of thinking, "I can do this, but it's going to be difficult," say to yourself, "It's going to be difficult, but I can do this." You want the last thing your brain hears to be positive.

✔ **Put yourself in the company of optimistic people.** Attitudes are contagious. Who do you know who sees the glass as half-full? That's the person you want to hang with!

✔ **Develop a personal action plan for reconstructing your attitude.** You're stuck in your negative thinking and you need to get unstuck.

20. Become a Hardy Person

Hardiness is a complex personality trait that is comprised of three essential elements. Hardy people:

- **Want control over their own lives:** Non-hardy people, on the other hand, depend more on luck, fate, chance, and the actions of other people — all things beyond their own control — to make the difference in how their lives go.

- **Are committed to the things and people that matter most to them:** Non-hardy people feel alienated and detached from the world around them. Hardy employees, for example, love their careers, while those lacking in hardiness see work as just a job.

- **Hardy people view life as a series of challenges:** Non-hardy people see life as "one damned thing after another."

Hardiness is more about actions (doing) than it is about attitude (thinking, feeling). Hardy people *do* the following types of things:

- Volunteer in the community

- Vote

- Show up at municipal government meetings

- Write letters to the editor of the local newspaper

- Get involved in their kids' activities

- Take classes at the community college, regardless of their age

- Share their opinions about important matters with others

- Look for jobs with new challenges and opportunities

- ✔ Become advocates for abused and neglected children
- ✔ Help get out the vote for their favorite political candidates
- ✔ Accept leadership positions
- ✔ Get regular health checkups
- ✔ Spend time with people they love
- ✔ Give to worthy charities
- ✔ Take on the tough challenges in life

This is just a list meant to illustrate the *types* of things hardy people do. You can be a hardy person and not go white-water rafting, or you can be a hardy person and not attend church. The common thread connecting all these types of activities is that you're actively doing them on a regular basis — and not just *thinking* about doing them.

21. Live an Honest Life

Conscientiousness is about truth, ethics, morality, being forthright and trustworthy, and having integrity. It's also about self-discipline. When you meet a conscientious person, what you see is what you get — there are no hidden agendas and, thus, no burdensome stress. You can never feel totally safe if you're living a lie — you're always on guard that someone will find out the truth.

If you aren't living an honest life, you can change. Here are some ways you can begin:

✔ **Stop apologizing for who and what you are.** If you're a scoundrel, admit it. If you're a decent person who fails to live up to someone else's expectations, let that be their problem — not yours.

✔ **Begin living your life as if it were, in fact, your own.** Make your own decisions and accept the consequences that follow. Always be open to advice from others, but don't take that as a mandate for how to live your life. If you do, you'll always blame them when things don't turn out in your favor.

✔ **Make sure your outer self matches up with your inner self.** Otherwise, you're, as they say, a house divided against itself.

✔ **Confess to yourself what's really behind all your anger and dissatisfaction.** In *Anger Management For Dummies,* I explain how easy this is to do.

✔ **Stop making excuses for not dealing with the part of life that's difficult or painful.** If you lack the courage to visit a dying friend in the hospital, just be honest and let her know that's how you feel. Don't try to tell yourself that you don't have the time or there are more important things that you need to do. Otherwise, head to the hospital and realize that it's a lot easier to live with your discomfort than it is to be dying.

22. Be Ethical

You can become a more ethical person if you:

✔ **Develop a set of principles to live by that conform to society's expectations.** For example, ascribing to the belief that "two wrongs never make a right" keeps you from answering bad behavior with more bad behavior.

✔ **Always try to put yourself in the other person's shoes.** If you wouldn't like someone to take advantage of you, then don't take advantage of him. If it upsets you when someone you trust lies to you, remember that when you're thinking about lying to someone else.

✔ **Deal with others in a straightforward manner.** Say what you think. The other person may not like it, but at least she knows where you stand.

✔ **Are consistent.** Don't tell one person something in one situation and then tell someone else just the opposite in another situation.

✔ **Seek to be righteous instead of always being right.** Being *right* means you say or do something that is technically correct. Being *righteous* is a virtue that's synonymous with being honorable, fair, and upstanding. The individual decides if he is right — society decides who is righteous.

23. Pursue What You Want, Not What You Have

If you're no longer happy with the status quo, here's what you need to do:

✔ **Explore life.** Don't be afraid to try new things — new foods, new vacation spots, or new types of reading material (the *Wall Street Journal* in place of your hometown newspaper). Take your mind and body to places they've never been before.

✔ **Question life.** If you're listening to the world news, don't just passively accept what the commentator says — question it: "Do I agree with what she's saying about the war in Iraq or not?"

✔ **Examine life.** Pay greater attention to what's going on around you and put all those meaningful issues in your life under your own microscope. Abortion, racism, affirmative action, gay parenting, and government-sponsored health insurance — none of these are simple issues and they need to be examined more closely before you decide how you feel about them.

✔ **Judge life.** Don't be afraid to make your own judgments about what constitutes right and wrong, fair and unfair, just and unjust, what will make you happy and unhappy — it's your right.

✔ **Ponder life's possibilities.** Don't just settle for life as the way it is — consider, "What if things were different?" Open your mind to alternative possibilities no matter what aspect of life you're dealing with.

✔ **Experience all of what life has to offer.** I had a lapel pin once that read "This is not a dress rehearsal." How true!

✔ **Let yourself feel — even when what you feel is uncomfortable.** You're wired to have lots of different emotions — joy, anger, fear, sadness. Emotions are your nervous system's way of communicating with you without using words. If you shut off the feelings, you shut off the messages behind them.

26

- **Learn to trust your feelings.** Intuition is a good thing. Your brain is telling you, "I've been in a similar situation before and here's what I think you should do right now."

- **Start looking at life as a glass half full rather than half empty.** Optimism always leads to hope; pessimism all too often leads to despair.

- **Seek diversity in all things.** Understanding diversity is really about understanding how each of us is unique.

- **Let curiosity reign.** Curiosity is the emotion that makes it easy for us to explore, question, examine, and ponder all of what life has to offer.

- **Quit holding back on passion.** If something makes you happy, let the world know it.

- **Stretch, moving beyond your usual comfort zone.** Every once in a while, try something unfamiliar, something more challenging than you're used to, or something without a predictable outcome.

24. Get into Flow: A Four-Step Process

We all need momentum to achieve things in life. These four steps can help.

Step 1: Identifying your sources of flow

Start with a list of skills you possess that have to do with sports, hobbies, career, socializing, and artistic endeavors.

After you've identified your skills, ask yourself three questions:

- ✔ When is the last time I did any of those things?

- ✔ Are there activities that I haven't gotten involved with before, but that I'd like to do?

- ✔ Am I letting my skills atrophy by not challenging them?

Step 2: Taking the plunge

Getting into flow is a process, and like any other process it has to have a beginning before it can have a middle and an end. Now is the time for action! Don't spend the rest of your life standing on the edge of the diving board being afraid to take the plunge — go ahead and make a splash!

Flow is about being so highly engaged in an activity that you lose track of time. Take off your watch when you're trying to get into flow — it only makes it easier to lose track of time when you don't know what time it is.

Step 3: Giving yourself enough time

Flow is a timeless state, but it does take a certain amount of time to get there. It's not something that you can hurry up.

Flow is about being so highly engaged in an activity that you lose track of time. Take off your watch when you're trying to get into flow — it only makes it easier to lose track of time when you don't know what time it is.

Step 4: Making flow a regular part of your day

People make all kinds of other things part of their regular day — including negative things like anger outbursts, substance abuse, a tedious and boring job, and hot-button relationships. Why not add in opportunities for getting into flow, being grateful, and doing things you enjoy doing?

 How can you enrich your day and get into flow? If you rarely or never experience flow, start by trying to make flow a part of your week. When you're getting into flow once a week, try upping it to three or four times a week. And then try making it a part of every day.

25. When Trouble Strikes, Ask Yourself Whether the Sky Really Is Falling

Unlike other animals, humans have the gift of perspective, and perspective is about choice! Having the right perspective is a key to achieving happiness and self improvement.

When tragedy strikes, most people initially feel as if there's no tomorrow. This response is nothing to be ashamed of — it just means we're human. The key is moving beyond that initial response and getting some perspective on the situation. To accomplish that, it helps to:

- ✔ **Think of what you've done in similar crisis situations in life.** Similar doesn't necessarily mean the same. For example, if you find yourself grappling with the bad news that you have prostate cancer, you might ask yourself "What did I do when I got fired from that job I had years ago — that I loved?" or "What did I do when my wife up and left me saying she didn't love me anymore?" After all, a crisis is a crisis — if the sky didn't fall the last time, it won't fall this time.

- ✔ **Recall what others have done in this same situation.** How did your brother react when he found out that he had cancer? If you're not sure, by all means call him up and ask him how he kept from panicking. Try looking at the sky from his perspective.

- ✔ **Think in non-catastrophic terms.** Instead of thinking "This is awful, terrible, horrible," say to yourself "This is bad — certainly not something I wanted to hear." Remember: Your brain listens to what you think as well as what you say — if you think the sky is falling, your brain will act as if it is and you will end up feeling overwhelmed.

26. Redirect Your Energies

Dealing with adversity takes a lot of energy — physical and psychological — especially when you see your circumstances as beyond your control. Initially, what little energy you have can easily end up being channeled into negative thoughts, feelings, and actions, which keep you from moving forward with your life.

✔ **Shift your time frame.** The benefit you're seeking has to do with the future, not the past. Sitting around ruminating or sulking about the past will only keep you "stuck" where you are — in a state of perpetual distress. Make sure your mind stays focused on the days, weeks, and months ahead. For example, "I'm going to run some errands for my wife this afternoon. I'm looking forward to spending time with my grandson later this week — I'll take him to the zoo. Next month is when we're going to the beach for a week — when I get down there, I don't seem to hurt as much."

✔ **Focus on what you can control, not on what you can't.** Ben was injured in a car accident and can't control his pain or get back all the things he lost because of it. What he could do instead is think about all the countless things he still can do that he's not doing because he's mired down in self-pity and regret (which are understandable, but nevertheless unproductive). Think *ability* rather than *disability* and, trust me, you'll feel a whole lot better!

✔ **Be productive in both thought and deed.** Reliving a trauma that happened to you years ago day after day is counter-productive if you're looking for a way to achieve a moment of happiness — all it does is bring back pain. Resisting all efforts to get you back into the mainstream of life is also counter-productive. Better to think "What can I do?" and then do it.

27. Forge Closer Ties to Those Around You

The vast majority of benefit that people find in the aftermath of misfortune comes from their interpersonal relationships — their connections to other people. People end up forging closer ties to those around them. How do they do that? They do it by taking the following advice:

✔ **When loved ones offer you support, accept it with appreciation instead of pushing it away.** This is no time for foolish pride which only keeps people at a distance. People want to help, so let them. And, always remember to say "thanks."

✔ **When others offer compassion and empathy, respond in kind.** Remember: You're not the only one in the world who's hurting in some way. People need you as much as you need them.

✔ **Educate others about your problem.** You have to tell your story in a way that helps those around you understand all of what you're going through and why you're meeting the challenge the way you are. Don't whine — educate!

✔ **Discover the kindness of strangers.** Friends often start out as strangers who want to help and the relationship evolves from there. If you turn away the kindness, you offend the person on the other end.

> ✔ **Foster better relationships with professionals whose help you need.** Doctors and lawyers (and, yes, psychologists) are human beings too — it never hurts to ask them "How are things with you? How's your son doing — I heard he was in an automobile accident?"

28. In the Face of Challenges, Revise Your Life Plan

Major life challenges involving trauma and loss disrupt your life and force you to redirect your energies, interests, and commitments. But how do you do that? It's not easy to revise your life and move into a positive, more satisfying future. But these steps can get you moving in the right direction:

1. **Create a positive mindset by sitting quietly with your eyes closed while opening your mind to the possibility of hope, optimism, and creative behavioral change.**

   Take ten exaggerated breaths, breathing in through your nose and out through your mouth while silently repeating the word *relax* each time you exhale.

2. **Identify a short list of valued life goals — for example, being closer to your family, becoming a more spiritual person, reconnecting with old friends.**

   Goals give you a sense of direction in terms of the changes you want to make. Basically, you're deciding what you want your life to stand for *from this point on.*

3. **Decide what the incentives are for you to reach these goals.**

What's the end game? Will you have greater peace of mind? Will you be happier? Will you live longer? Will you feel less alone with your suffering? Will you have a new lease on life? Be specific.

4. **Ask yourself how committed you are to achieving each goal.**

The more committed you are, the more successful you'll be.

5. **Ask yourself how *confident* you are about making these changes.**

Commitment and confidence are not the same. You can be committed, but not all that confident — or, the other way around.

6. **Consider what specific things you would need to realize each goal.**

Where would you start? How much support do you need? If you have several goals, which one do you begin with? Make it easy on yourself — start with the smallest, easiest thing and work your way up to the big changes.

7. **Identify any obstacles to meet your objectives.**

Do you have physical limitations that might interfere? Is depression a problem? Are other people's attitudes holding you back?

8. **Decide how you're going to overcome those obstacles.**

For example, get professional help for your depression.

9. **Begin — just start.**

It doesn't matter what you do; the important thing is that you just do something.

Change takes effort, so you have to persist, even when the going gets tough. There's no easy way to accomplish change. Change also takes time, so be patient. As the saying goes, "Rome wasn't built in a day." You can't a reconstruct your life in a day either. Focus on the destination, but enjoy the journey.

10. **Reward yourself for whatever changes you make no matter how small.**

If change is rewarding, keep at it — if it isn't, quit. It's just that simple!

29. Have a Heart-to-Heart with a Higher Power

The peace and tranquility that comes from a belief in a power greater than oneself is an antidote to unhappiness and the doubt and uncertainty that accompanies unexpected, unwanted changes in life. The nature of that higher power is not as important as the meaningful social tie you have to that entity.

In order for prayer to work, you need to be honest in your conversation with your higher power. This is not the time to hold back. Admit your fears, your anger, and your feeling of vulnerability, and ask for help. Recognize that you're a human being — no more, no less — not some invincible, superpower who can handle everything that life throws at you. This is what humility is all about.

Prayer is an act of faith, and faith can be a weapon that helps you survive unhappy times. Take a few minutes each day and have a quiet conversation with a higher power. The nature of the prayer doesn't matter. It can be a prayer of uncertainty ("Lord, I've lost my sense of direction and don't know where to go from here"), a prayer of solicitation ("God, please grant me the courage to see this through"), or a prayer of desperation ("God, I feel so lost and alone"). The simple act of having faith is what's empowering.

30. Know How to Begin and End Each Day

Coherence comes from structure, and when that structure — those routine, meaningful activities that make you feel like you're on top of life — is disturbed, you must slowly but surely replace that structure, which is not always an easy task.

New routines are best developed by concentrating on the beginning and end of each day. Let the middle of the day take care of itself. Focus on tasks that meet the three M's test — that is, something that makes sense, is manageable (within your power to do), and is meaningful. And keep it simple!

Here are some ways you may want to start and end your day:

- ✔ Spending a few minutes in quiet prayer
- ✔ Doing 20 minutes of light exercise
- ✔ Taking your dog for a walk

- ✔ Having breakfast at a restaurant where you're considered a regular
- ✔ Sending e-mails to close friends and wishing them a pleasant day
- ✔ Spending 15 minutes in meditation
- ✔ Feeding the birds in your yard
- ✔ Having a neighbor over for coffee
- ✔ Having a conversation with someone who cares about you

Start and end your day the same way every day. These routines can be the building blocks for a renewed sense of coherence.

31. Count Your Opportunities and Blessings

In an effort to achieve a more positive, confident mindset as you go through the day, be aware of all the opportunities life offers you as well as the blessings that come your way.

Begin and end each day reminding yourself of at least ten ways in which your life has been blessed. Do you feel blessed with good health? Are you blessed by having people in your life who love and care for you? Are you blessed with certain talents and skills that not everyone else has? Are you blessed with children who are good citizens and are succeeding at life? Everyone has something in his life he can be thankful for.

32. Find Meaning

Viktor Frankl's wonderful book *Man's Search for Meaning* (Washington Square Press) makes a cogent argument for how a person can only achieve happiness through a life with purpose. That sense of purpose, he suggests, can come from one of three sources:

- ✔ Some type of creative or constructive work or deed
- ✔ Intimate, loving relationships
- ✔ Rising above some tragic life circumstance (in Frankl's case, the horrors of life in a German concentration camp)

A life that includes none of these three elements is, according to Frankl, empty and meaningless. And it is a life rife with unhappiness in the form of depression, violence, and addiction.

How have you managed to find meaning in your life? Today is a good day to start creating your meaning in life. Here's how: Find an activity where you can forget about yourself and focus more on the needs of others — for example, becoming involved in the Big Brother/Big Sister program and doing what you can to enhance the life of a child. Find an activity that has more to do with your character — compassionate, entertaining — than your profession or career — psychologist, electrician. Think of someone you admire and start doing some of those things they do. Look around for things that everyone agrees should be done, but no one wants to do — and you be the one to do them. All of us look at the trash littering our highways and think "I wish somebody would pick that stuff up." Why don't you be that somebody and make the rest of us happy?

33. Think Positive Thoughts

Over the years, a lot has been written and said about the power of positive thinking. All of it is based on the premise that what's in your head — positive thoughts — inevitably influences what's in your heart as well as how you behave.

Here are some examples of the kind of positive thoughts that can lead to happiness:

- This is such a lovely day.
- There really are nice people in the world — like the driver who let me pull in front of him so that I could turn at the light.
- My partner is such a thoughtful person.
- I'm not rich, but I'm thankful that I have enough to pay my bills.
- I'm a very healthy person for my age.
- I love it when I hear the birds start to sing — it means spring is on the way.
- That massage felt wonderful!
- It's always great to hear from my kids — even when they have a problem.
- If I could live my life all over again, I wouldn't change a thing.

 Carry a notebook with you and write down every positive thought you have in a given day. Sometimes at the end of a long day it's hard to remember all the positives you experienced, but if you write them down throughout the day, you'll be able to reread your list before you go to bed and remind yourself that the day was actually pretty good.

34. Feel Positive Feelings

Happiness is not just about feeling joyful. It comes from other positive feelings that you and I experience in the course of everyday life as well. In essence, one good feeling leads to another. If you have enough of these other positive emotions, you can't help but be happy.

What positive feelings have you experienced lately? Here are some examples:

- ✔ Awed
- ✔ Content
- ✔ Comfortable
- ✔ Compassionate
- ✔ Connected (as opposed to lonely)
- ✔ Generous
- ✔ Grateful
- ✔ Excited
- ✔ Satisfied
- ✔ Serene
- ✔ Upbeat

Use this list as a starting point, and write down any *positive* feelings you've had in the past 24 hours. If you have trouble identifying very many positive feelings, that's a heads-up that you may be paying too much attention to the negative emotions or, in fact, that you simply aren't feeling anything positive. Doing this exercise daily will help you become more aware of positive feelings that are there — just unnoticed. If you aren't having any positive feelings at all, day after day, then you probably need to get some professional help in figuring out why not — even mildly depressed people can feel upbeat and excited.

35. Take Positive Actions

It's not always what you think and feel that makes you happy as much as it is what you actually *do* in the course of a given day. When you're making your daily confession, try to think of all the positive things you did in the past 24 hours.

Here are some examples of positive actions:

- ✔ Held the door open for an elderly person at the post office.
- ✔ Slammed on the brakes to keep from running over a dog in the road.
- ✔ Picked up litter along the roadside.
- ✔ Returned a wallet I found in the parking lot to its rightful owner.
- ✔ Sent a get-well card to an ailing friend.
- ✔ Did the dishes so that my partner wouldn't have to do them after work.
- ✔ Said "thank you" to everyone who helped me throughout the day.
- ✔ Took time to go to the gym to exercise.
- ✔ Treated a friend to lunch.

- ✔ Went to bed early and got a good night's sleep for a change.
- ✔ Bought my partner some flowers.

36. Keep a Journal

If you take just 15 or 20 minutes a day and write down everything positive you can think of that happened during the day, you'll see on a daily basis how much you have to be thankful for. This journal is for your eyes only, to remind you of what you have to be thankful for or happy about.

Don't think of this as a diary — you're not going to keep it after you're done. Here are some things to keep in mind as you write your happiness journal:

- ✔ **Make yourself the audience.** You're writing this to yourself. It's a private conversation — you're not trying to impress anyone or to make someone else feel better. Fill the pages with self-references — words like *I* and *me*. Writing in the first person makes it a *personal* conversation between you and yourself, as opposed to a conversation between you and someone else. It also makes *you* responsible for the positive thoughts, emotions, and actions you write about.

- ✔ **Forget the grammar.** This is one writing exercise where grammar doesn't matter. You don't have to be an English major to confess how good you feel at the end of the day. Just write from the heart. Write without thinking too much — let your writing be spontaneous. No one is going to grade you, so you can forget the rules.

✔ **Write until time's up.** Give yourself the full 15 to 20 minutes to complete this exercise. Don't be in a hurry to make your confession. Enjoy it! The exercise itself should make you feel better, so make it last. If it helps, set a kitchen timer and write until you hear the bell — and, then just stop even if you're in the middle of a sentence.

✔ **After you're done writing, read what you wrote.** Circle all the positive feelings you wrote about — like *happy, excited,* and *relaxed.* Underline all of the positive *thoughts* you wrote down (for example, "I reminded myself how fortunate I was to have a college education"). Put a checkmark next to each positive *action* you took during the day. Now add up all those notations. Paying attention to the positive feelings, thoughts, and actions you wrote about will give you a sense of whether you're getting a good balance of all three in your day.

This daily exercise serves as an active reminder of the fact that you're probably having a better day than you realize.

37. Engage in Group Confessions

When my wife and I get together for dinner with our Friday night friends, we don't sit around and complain about all our problems. Instead, we share all the positive things that are going on in our lives. We confess to each other the good news, not just the bad. We try to uplift one another in order to end the week on a positive note. I announce that "We finally sold our office building and now I can retire." A younger member of our group, who has recently started a business of his own, tells us about a new contract he's landed that will earn him a lot of money. His wife, who makes handbags for a living, talks about the successful show she had in a nearby city the past weekend. Another member of the group updates us on how well her daughter is doing in law school and how much she enjoys living in Florida. And so it goes. (Don't get me wrong: If someone has a problem, of course, everyone will hear them out and offer support. It's just that we don't want Friday night to become a group therapy experience.)

If you're not already involved in a regular group meeting with family and friends, where the conversation is upbeat and focuses on the good stuff, start your own group. The size of the group isn't important — what matters is the character of the people (you want to choose optimists over pessimists) and the content of the conversation.

If you're going to gossip about other people, make sure it's positive gossip. Say *good* things behind their backs! For example, "Did you hear about Sally? She got that job she applied for? Isn't that wonderful. I'm so happy for her." Sally won't know what you said, but *you* will.

38. Identify Who or What Makes You Smile

Think about what a smile does for you. It attracts people. It says to the world "I'm a happy, confident, competent, satisfied person." It makes it easier to build a support network — people who will rally to your side when adversity strikes. It helps you transcend difficult times.

I don't want to say that most people are clueless when it comes to knowing who and what makes them happy, but it *is* true that people's understanding of the relationship between life circumstances and positive emotion is not as precise as it should be.

One simple, easy way to identify your particular sources of happiness is to rummage through old photographs and cull out the ones where you're smiling. Some of those will no doubt be pictures of family gatherings where everyone is posing for the camera — looking happy for the camera's sake whether you feel that way or not. But other pictures may capture moments of genuine happiness, as evidenced by the Duchenne smile on your face.

Examine those photographs carefully and ask yourself what the common threads are that connect them. For example, maybe whenever you're in the company of certain people or whenever you're engaged in some particular activity, you're smiling. What you're looking for here is a pattern — something that repeats itself. (In every picture where I'm with my wife, my children, my dogs, or special friends, I have a smile on my face — except for those years where I was struggling with depression, and then nothing made me smile.)

39. Start with a Smile and Go from There

Put a smile on your face and hold it for 20 or 30 seconds and then relax your face. Repeat this smiling exercise 10 to 20 times and see if you don't suddenly feel more positive. Better yet, do this exercise in front of a mirror so that you can experience what psychologists call *facial feedback* — that is, your emotions begin to conform to your facial features. Assume that somewhere in your psyche there is this thing called happiness; the smile you're putting on your face is just a way of letting it out.

The smile exercise is no different than any other form of exercise. The more you do it, the easier it gets. What begins as contrived eventually becomes natural.

40. Be Generous, but Give the Right Way

If you act generously to others, shouldn't you experience the "joy of giving"? It depends. If there is a positive motive behind your generosity — for example, compassion — the answer is "yes." If, on the other hand, your generosity is motivated by a sense of obligation on your part or a need to control others, then the answer is decidedly "no." In other words, there's a right way to give and a wrong way to give — one way leads to happiness, the other does not.

If you're going to be generous, make sure it's for the right reason. Doing for others because you feel you *have to* rather than because you *want to* will not make you happy. Stick to giving because you want to, and you'll never go wrong.

When you give, you need to give without strings attached — you need to be generous without any expectation of reciprocity or payback. True gifts are one-way transactions. They aren't made out of a sense of obligation, nor do they obligate the recipient.

41. Increase Your Uplifts

How do you increase your uplifts? Simple: You do little things that bring you pleasure. You don't just wait passively to be uplifted — you make it happen! For example, you can lift your spirits by:

- Treating yourself to a delicious dessert in the middle of the afternoon.
- Spending your lunch hour sunning yourself on a park bench.
- Taking 20 minutes to meditate.
- Taking time to feed the birds who visit your yard before going off to work.
- Watching children at play.
- Daydreaming about positive experiences you've had in the past.
- Giving yourself permission to have that extra cup of coffee before you join the "rat race."
- Enjoying a glass of wine at an outdoor café.
- Listening to some of your favorite songs while you drive from point A to point B.
- Reading a magazine article about something that interests you.

These are all things that you can initiate. They don't depend on what other people are willing or able to do that might please you. They're things that you have control over.

42. Recognize the Importance of Rituals

Much of everyday life is made up of *rituals* — established, predictable, patterned behaviors that structure the day. There are morning rituals (brushing your teeth, showering, reading the newspaper), midday rituals (everything from the so-called "power lunch" to a simple baloney sandwich in your office), and evening rituals (a cocktail or two, dinner at 6 p.m., a few minutes of intimate conversation with your spouse, and — if you're lucky — sex).

Rituals are a form of structure that actually make life flow more easily. They're mindless — you do them without thinking. Perhaps most important of all, they orient you as to where you are and what you should be doing. Rituals are like an invisible watch — if you're taking a shower, it must be morning! Without rituals, every day is a new day full of unpredictability, uncertainty, and the possibility of unhappiness.

Here are some examples of what I'm talking about — rituals you can incorporate into your life (if you haven't already):

- ✔ Exercising first thing in the morning
- ✔ Sitting for a few minutes of quiet contemplation, in meditation or prayer
- ✔ Getting a professional massage once a month
- ✔ Browsing through your favorite bookstore every Saturday morning
- ✔ Checking in via e-mail with loved ones once a day

- ✔ Taking an afternoon nap
- ✔ Enjoying some quality, one-on-one time with your pet
- ✔ Spending five minutes every day reflecting on all the things you have to be grateful for

Don't become a slave to rituals; otherwise, they become tedious. If something more interesting comes along at the same time you normally take your afternoon nap, go for it! You can always nap tomorrow.

43. Spend More Time Doing Absolutely Nothing

Some people simply can't comprehend the psychological benefit that comes from doing absolutely nothing — nothing that's productive, that is, in a material or tangible sense like building things or making money. On the other hand, when you do nothing, you *produce* a state of relaxation. Funny how that works!

Here are some tips on how to spend more time doing nothing:

- ✔ Rent a dozen of your favorite movies and spend the entire weekend watching them. Your kids will love you!
- ✔ Get up on Saturday morning and head out for the day without any particular agenda or destination. If something along the road to nowhere catches your eye, stop.
- ✔ Spend the whole day reading your favorite novel — lose yourself in the author's world.

✔ Plan a weekend so that when you go to work on Monday morning and people ask you what you did, you can say, with a smile on your face, "Absolutely nothing!"

✔ Lose your watch. It's much easier to do nothing if you don't know what time it is.

44. Set Priorities

Some families have priorities — things that they feel are most important and crucial to family life and success and that give the family a clearly defined sense of direction and purpose. Other families do not — they're like tumbleweeds, blowing this way and that and getting nowhere in particular.

Try this exercise to help your family set its own priorities:

1. **Find a time when the whole family can sit down together for at least an hour.**

2. **Pass out sheets of paper and ask each family member to write down three priorities he or she thinks the family has or should have.**

   Give examples like the ones I mention earlier in this section. Also, mention things like honesty, supporting each other, and health. Emphasize that this is not about your individual priorities — it's about what you think the family should be doing as a group.

3. **Then, one by one, have each member do a "show and tell," sharing his list and explaining why he chose the things he did.**

4. **Don't comment right away — wait until everyone has shared their list and then open the door for discussion.**

Are there any points of agreement — things listed by more than one family member? Are there any glaring omissions? Do family members see any obstacles to achieving these priorities? Is there anyone in the family who seems to not want to get onboard with these priorities? If so, don't criticize them; instead say "It's okay if you don't want to share you priorities with us now, but we really do want to know what you think this family should be doing more of that we aren't or less of than we are." Leave the door open for them to join in later on.

The goal is to end the hour with a firm sense of what you value as a family.

45. Indulge Your Alternative Self

I believe that each person has two selves:

- ✔ **The primary self,** which dominates everyday life and is there for all to see

- ✔ **The alternative self,** which is not always free to express itself

Take a pad of paper and make two lists describing both your primary and alternative selves. Describe each self by using adjectives — for example, *industrious, cheerful, cynical, happy-go-lucky, adventurous, conservative,* and so on. How different are the two lists? How often do you indulge your alternative self? Does it take something like alcohol to release the side of you that most people don't know? Are you the only one who knows your alternative self — do you only act silly when no one else is around?

46. Be More Balanced

In general, the people who can't seem to pull themselves away from work and are highly stressed are Type-A personalities. And the people who are a bit more laid back and relaxed are Type B's. To understand why Type A's spend so much time working and too little time playing, you have to see the world from their perspective and contrast that with the perspective of Type B's.

Type A versus Type B

Type A People	Type B People
Have a rigid standard for what constitutes satisfactory performance. They're continually striving to meet some illusory goal of perfection.	Demand less from themselves even though they fully intend to meet the requirements of the job. They settle for being a "good employee" rather than striving to be a "perfect employee."
Feel the need to engage in multiple tasks at the same time, giving each task number-one priority.	Are more satisfied completing one task at a time before moving on to the next one. They tend to prioritize tasks, ranking them as more or less important.

(continued)

Type A versus Type B *(continued)*

Type A People	Type B People
View work as a competitive enterprise. They often initiate competition in noncompetitive situations. The word *cooperation* isn't in their vocabulary.	Make good team players. They aren't averse to healthy competition but enjoy working collaboratively with others.
Prefer working alone but end up feeling like they carry the burden of getting the job done squarely on their shoulders.	Are quick to share the responsibility of work assignments so that they don't become burdensome.

If you see yourself in that Type A column, you can make a few key changes in your life to adopt some more of the Type B tendencies. Here are a few ideas:

✔ Appreciate the arts

✔ Be curious

✔ Put down the grade book

✔ Lose the watch

✔ Eat slowly

✔ Think of others as just as important as yourself

✔ Take your time

✔ Eliminate number-speak

47. Develop Meaningful Social Ties

Human beings are social creatures. We're also wired for emotions, and we experience those emotions within a social context. We're at our best when we're engaging one another in the course of daily activities — at work and at play. If those activities are productive, constructive, involve mutual cooperation, and contribute to our ultimate survival, we tend to feel joyful, happy, and satisfied. If they're unproductive, destructive, or involve conflict, we feel just the opposite — anxious, resentful, and dissatisfied. What's important is the nature of your relationships and the extent to which they're supportive.

Being socially "connected" to the world around you benefits you in two major ways: It keeps you healthy and it makes life more fun.

You may find yourself at a point in life where you have no one to confide in — no one to talk to about the important things that are going on in your life, to assist you in overcoming obstacles, or to simply "give you a voice." If this is the case, you need to begin reaching out — go where the people are and let them get to know you. Become a volunteer, find a hobby club to join, or show up the next time they have a young member's event at your local art museum or Fine Arts Center.

People don't start out to be confidants — they start out just getting to know one another, and things progress from there. If you've already tried that and still feel unconnected, I highly recommend filling that need through some type of counseling relationship — for example, with a mental health practitioner or a member of the clergy. Not only is there no shame in that, it's the wise, smart, and right thing to do!

48. Get Enough Support

Support, according to sociologist James House at the University of Michigan, involves "a flow of one or more of four types of support between people." These four types of support are

- ✔ **Emotional support:** You need to know that people are in your corner. You need others to tell you "I'm here for you no matter what."

- ✔ **Informational support:** You need information, guidance, and advice about what to do or how to handle situations. People who can give you this kind of support include lawyers, clergy members, physicians, mental health professionals, and accountants.

- ✔ **Tangible support:** This is the chicken-soup type of support. Tangible support includes things like a ride to the doctor's office, a loan of money, help moving to another house, and watching your children so that you and your partner can enjoy a much needed night out on the town.

- ✔ **Appraisal support:** You need someone to give you honest, frank, constructive feedback about yourself — for example, that you never seem happy any more. This is not the type of support that typically comes from strangers or from acquaintances.

49. Take Solitude Seriously

You don't need to talk most people into socializing — after all, humans are social animals. But solitude is another matter. Solitude runs counter to the demands of society, which depends on the efforts of all of us to contribute to the greater good. Taking time for yourself is often viewed as selfish and unproductive.

Solitude is also uncomfortable for many people because they've learned to derive their self-esteem from activities initiated by their "other selves" — that is, their efforts to satisfy themselves by satisfying others. Your "other self" includes such roles as child, student, sibling, grandchild, Girl Scout, athlete, employee, employer, church deacon, neighbor, and citizen. When you serve your "other self," you achieve some measure of happiness — true — but there are also important benefits that come from spending time with your "personal self," that part of you that doesn't need other people to be happy.

✔ **Solitude allows your brain to rest.** In a world of overstimulation, our minds are constantly in an overactive mode. Solitude allows your mind to detach from all the endless chatter coming from the environment around you — the radio, the Internet, conversations, street noise, traffic sounds, barking dogs — and rest for a change.

✔ **Solitude enhances creativity.** Solitude frees the mind up from all the distractions of everyday life and allows it to focus more fully on one thing. It allows your brain to think outside the box and to come up with unique, extraordinary solutions to ordinary problems. That's part of why artists —

painters, sculptures, musicians, writers — spend so much time alone.

✔ **Solitude can be a time of self-discovery.** Solitude is your chance to learn something about yourself. Self-discovery is a process that involves asking and answering four basic questions:

- Who am I?
- What makes me unique?
- Where am I going in life?
- Am I comfortable with myself?

✔ **Solitude provides an opportunity for perspective.** When you're caught up in the hassles of day-to-day life, all you can see is what's directly in front of you — the problem of the moment. If you want to see and appreciate the big picture of what your life's all about, you have to step back and get a bird's-eye view — and that's exactly what solitude allows you to do.

50. Love What You Do

Do you love your work or your day-to-day routine? If not, consider the following:

✔ **Don't think of your job as an all-or-nothing thing.** Break it down into its various components — meetings, sales, dealing with subordinates — and focus on those activities that you enjoy most. That's where you should be spending most of your time.

✔ **Think of your work relative to the other aspects of your lifestyle.** Sometimes work can provide escape from the stresses of home and family life.

✔ **Consider the alternatives — if you weren't doing this, what would you be doing?** Believe it or not, no matter how much you dislike your job, there's always something worse out there!

✔ **Try to assign meaning to your work that goes beyond the routine aspects of your job description.** All companies have a mission statement — find out what yours is and be part of that mission.

✔ **Get those parts of your job that you don't love behind you early in the day.** From there on out, it's all downhill.

✔ **Act as though you love what you do, even if you don't.** That's right, fake it! Empower yourself by putting a smile on your face.

✔ **Find a compatriot, a fellow traveler as you journey through the work day, preferably someone who loves her work more than you do.** Who knows? Maybe her optimism and enthusiasm will prove contagious.

✔ **Start looking for a new job if you've tried everything you can think of to be happy at work and nothing works.** Be optimistic and tell yourself that there's a job out there somewhere that suits you better.

Want more?

Visit **www.dummies.com/go/target** to get related articles, videos, or illustrated step-by-steps on your favorite Dummies title.

Guitar
ALL-IN-ONE

FOR DUMMIES

8 BOOKS IN 1

• Guitar For Dummies, 2nd Edition
• Rock Guitar For Dummies
• Blues Guitar For Dummies
• Classical Guitar For Dummies
• Guitar Exercises For Dummies
• Songwriting For Dummies
• Music Composition For Dummies
• Music Theory For Dummies

Superfoods
FOR **DUMMIES**

Learn to:

• Purchase and prepare extremely healthy foods
• Improve your diet and live longer
• Increase your energy and control your weight
• Prevent disease and avoid costly trips to the doctor

Brent Agin, MD
Coauthor, Healthy Aging For Dummies
Shereen Jegtvig, MS

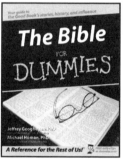

Your guide to the Good Book's stories, history, and influence

The Bible
FOR **DUMMIES**

Jeffrey Geoghegan, PhD
Michael Homan, PhD

A Reference for the Rest of Us!®

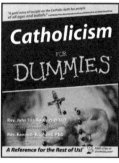

"A gold mine of insight on the Catholic faith for people of all ages and beliefs."

Catholicism
FOR **DUMMIES**

Rev. John Trigilio Jr., PhD, ThD
Rev. Kenneth Brighenti, PhD

A Reference for the Rest of Us!®
FREE eTips at dummies.com®

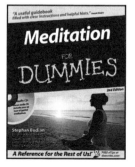

"A useful guidebook filled with clear instructions and helpful hints."

Meditation
FOR **DUMMIES**

2nd Edition

Stephan Bodian

A Reference for the Rest of Us!®
FREE eTips at dummies.com®

Your book can give you reduced stress, better relations, and living a more fulfilling life

Happiness
FOR **DUMMIES**

W. Doyle Gentry, PhD

A Reference for the Rest of Us!®
FREE eTips at dummies.com®

Making Everything Easier!™

4th Edition

Personal Finance

FOR DUMMIES

Learn to:
- Assess your financial fitness
- Save more and spend less
- Review your credit report and improve your score
- Make smart investments in any economic environment

Eric Tyson, MBA
Bestselling author, Investing For Dummies

Now updated! The bestselling guide to managing diabetes
featuring coverage of the latest treatments

Diabetes

FOR DUMMIES

3rd Edition

Alan L. Rubin, MD

A Reference for the Rest of Us!™

Covers the iPhone, iPhone 3G, and iPhone 3G S!

3rd Edition

iPhone

FOR DUMMIES

Learn to:
- Set up your iPhone, send and receive e-mail, and browse the Internet
- Shoot great videos and take and share photos
- Use GPS maps, listen to music, and download your favorite apps

IN FULL COLOR!

Edward C. Baig
Bob "Dr. Mac" LeVitus

Making Everything Easier!™

4th Edition

iPod & iTunes

FOR DUMMIES

Learn to:
- Set up iTunes and your iPod
- Shop at the iTunes Store
- Manage photos and videos on your iPod
- Add music tracks from a CD to your iTunes library

Tony Bove

Want more?

Visit **www.dummies.com/go/target** to get related articles, videos, or illustrated step-by-steps on your favorite Dummies title.

With more than 1,600 titles to choose from, we've got a Dummies book for wherever you are in life! Look for Dummies titles wherever books are sold, call 877-762-2974 or visit *dummies.com*.